GET $mart WITH YOUR MONEY™

FIRST Job
SMARTS

P9-DYB-703

Daniel E. Harmon

ROSEN
PUBLISHING®
New York

Published in 2010 by The Rosen Publishing Group, Inc.
29 East 21st Street, New York, NY 10010

First Edition

Library of Congress Cataloging-in-Publication Data

Harmon, Daniel E.
First job smarts / Daniel E. Harmon.—1st ed.
    p. cm.—(Get smart with your money)
Includes bibliographical references and index.
ISBN-13: 978-1-4358-5268-6 (library binding)
ISBN-13: 978-1-4358-5542-7 (pbk)
ISBN-13: 978-1-4358-5543-4 (6 pack)
1. Teenagers—Employment—Juvenile literature. 2. Part time employment—
Juvenile literature. 3. Teenagers—Finance, Personal—Juvenile literature.
I. Title.
HD6270.H37 2010
650.1—dc22

                                                    2008042892

Manufactured in Malaysia

Contents

Introduction

Everyone knows how to spend money. Not everyone knows how to spend it wisely. Not everyone understands the importance of saving and investing either. A first job presents a wonderful opportunity for you to "get smart" with money. In fact, you quickly see that money management is not just a good idea; it's a requirement.

Until your mid-teens, you get most of your money from your parents. You may receive a weekly allowance. Your parents may pay you to do household chores. If money is given to you, you tend to be less careful with it than if you have to work for it. Your spending habits usually improve after you get your first job. You remember how much time and effort went into each paycheck. It becomes important to you not to waste your hard-earned money.

Teenagers want money for a lot of things: new clothes, entertainment, cool new cell phones. Sometimes, they look for odd jobs to earn money for special desires: a summer trip, a musical instrument, a new bike. Some young workers find jobs because they need to help support their families. Others want to begin saving for long-term objectives: college, a car, a trip to Europe after high school graduation. A few have a definite career path in

A fifteen-year-old server at an ice cream stand tops a concoction with confetti. A side benefit of many such jobs is that workers can eat for free or at reduced prices.

mind, and they look for a job that will help launch them in that direction.

Before they enter the nation's official workforce—before they even enter high school—teenagers can earn money. Some make all the money they want babysitting, shoveling snow, walking dogs, tutoring, teaching guitar, or performing in a rock band. But as they reach the minimum employment age in their states, many teenagers begin to look for regular jobs.

Most jobs that are available for you are in retail businesses. Chain restaurants, for example, hire young cooks and cashiers. Supermarkets and other stores need checkout, bagging, and stock workers. The pay for most of these jobs is minimum wage or slightly higher. It is difficult for an adult to make a living at minimum wage. For you, though, these earnings can be exciting. The young worker not only has spending money but can also begin to save and even invest.

Also important is the experience. Prior work histories will prove very valuable later, when you graduate from high school or college and begin a career.

Any first job is a thrill. It provides a sense of worth, not to mention the pay. Whatever the job is, the first-time employee should recognize it as a great learning experience. You see exactly how money comes and goes. Hopefully, you are becoming money smart. Good money management involves many things. It means learning how to prepare a budget, how to spend wisely, how to save and invest for the future, how to satisfy the laws, and how to help improve society.

The workaday world is a world of demands and expectations, regular hours, and important tasks to perform. It is also where money is made—money that must be handled wisely.

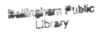
CHAPTER 1
Basic Requirements for Young Job Seekers

To obtain a regular, salaried job, you must meet certain requirements. The job itself will have requirements. Besides a minimum age, it may involve driving. Do you have a license and a vehicle? It may require typing, math, and good communication skills. You may have to take a drug test and undergo vaccinations. The employer may insist that a worker have no criminal record and may request school records. Some medical conditions and disabilities might prevent a person from performing a job satisfactorily. Practically all employers require references; most employers actually contact them to ask about the character of the applicant. Government requirements also must be met.

Paperwork

Every American worker (and citizens who do not work, too) should have a Social Security number and a Social Security card. Many children have Social Security cards and do not realize it. When they were born, their parents may have applied for their Social Security number at the hospital, at the same time that they applied for a birth

Your Social Security card is an extremely important, private item. You should memorize your Social Security number and keep the card in a safe place.

certificate. If so, the parents probably are keeping the child's card in a safe place. The child should not sign and use the card until 1) he or she reaches the age of eighteen or 2) begins work, if that occurs at an earlier age.

People who have never been issued a Social Security card can apply for it by visiting the nearest Social Security office or online. (See www.socialsecurity.gov/online/ss-5.html.) They must provide proof of identity and proof of U.S. citizenship.

Citizens are advised not to carry their Social Security cards in person. Rather, they should store them in secure places. If a purse or wallet is stolen and it contains the victim's Social

Security card, the theft of that very private information can cause big problems.

Social Security is the system by which workers pay money into a government program throughout their working lives. The amount they pay in determines the amount they can receive back later. When they retire, or if they become disabled before retirement, their investment in the Social Security program can bring them regular government payments to provide income in difficult times.

Some states (not the federal government) require workers under the age of eighteen to obtain employment certificates and age certificates. These are called work papers. School guidance counselors can tell you whether or not these are required. They can probably furnish the forms you need to fill out, or tell you how to obtain forms from the state government. Work papers typically require you to obtain a basic physical fitness checkup by a doctor and provide proof of age (birth certificate, driver's license, etc.). A parent or guardian's assistance may be required.

Résumés, Cover Letters, and Interviews

You, a new job seeker, should begin by preparing a résumé. This document tells employers basic information about you, with an emphasis on special skills, previous experience, and personal interests. The résumé is an essential tool that you will update regularly and keep handy until retirement. The longer a person works, gains new experience, and obtains advanced education, the longer and more impressive the résumé will become.

There are different types of résumés. If you are a person with no work experience, you should develop what's called a

John Doe
111 Main Street
Cleveland, OH
555.555.5555

jdoe@ispservices.com

Objective: To obtain a position in an auto parts store and begin a career in the parts business

Summary of Qualifications
• Broad knowledge of auto repair and parts
• Excellent customer relations skills
• Ability to work under pressure
• Willingness to work hard

Relevant Experience
2006–present: Bob's Burgers, Cleveland
• Wait on customers
• Cook and prepare food orders in fast-paced environment
• Advanced from cook to assistant manager in 18 months

2003–present: Repair cars
• Perform minor repairs and tune-ups
• Rebuilt engine of Ford Mustang

Education
Roosevelt High School, Cleveland, OH
Classes in auto mechanics

Your first résumé probably will contain only basic information about you. As you obtain work experience, your résumé will grow longer and more impressive.

functional résumé. Since you do not have previous jobs to describe, this résumé focuses on your skills and interests.

Once you have on-the-job experience, a chronological résumé may be more effective. This type presents your employment history job by job, beginning with the most recent. It can show how you are progressing in a particular career or area of experience.

Your name, address, phone number, and e-mail address appear at the top of the résumé. Usually, the body of the résumé begins with a brief statement of "objective." Your overall objective in finding a job might be to serve a certain segment of the buying public. It may be to help people with special needs. It may be to protect the environment or improve the community. It may be to advance in the restaurant or hotel industries, drive a truck for a major distributing company, or sell houses. It may be to make furniture or clothes, write for a newspaper, or work with animals.

The résumé will then list your skills, any previous experience, and your education. It should let the employer know why you are a good candidate for a specific job. At the end, you should provide the names and contact information of at least three references. These are people who can recommend you for a job. (It is important to get their permission before naming them as references.)

When applying for a job in person, you should bring a copy of the résumé for the employer to review and place on file. When applying by letter or e-mail, you should enclose the résumé and a brief cover letter. The cover letter should have a catchy first sentence that gets the employer's attention. Busy employers may not spend more than a few seconds scanning a cover letter unless they immediately read something about the applicant that attracts them. For example, the letter should never begin, "I would like to apply for your advertised job as a

Seven Tips for Teenage Job Hunters

1. Start writing your résumé. Even if you have little or no work experience and your résumé contains nothing more than your personal interests and contact information, it's the launching pad for your first job and your future career. Include even small jobs—pet sitting, yard maintenance, babysitting—in your first résumé.

2. Commit yourself to finishing high school. In most career fields, a higher education will lead to higher and faster advancement. At the least, you will need a high school diploma to find a wide choice of interesting job opportunities.

3. Let employed friends know you are interested in a part-time job while you're a student. They can tell you of openings where they work and point you to the hiring official. They also can explain what they like and dislike about their jobs.

4. Learn all you can about a job before you apply. If it isn't something you can or want to do, it will be embarrassing to find that out after you're hired.

5. Don't be late for a job interview, even by a minute.

6. Let the job interviewer know you're eager to join the team. Be able to explain why you prefer to work there—and nowhere else.

7. Don't be discouraged if, after an interview, you don't get a job offer. If you've made a good impression, the interviewer may call you when another opening comes up later.

sales assistant." The employer may read no further. A much more effective opening would be, "I am eager to join your team as a sales assistant and help your business grow."

Most employers have applications for aspiring workers to fill out before an interview. Some applications lead to nothing; they are filed away, perhaps unread, and are eventually destroyed. If the employer is impressed by the application, the cover letter, and the résumé, the applicant will be called in for an interview when an appropriate job opening arises. First impressions are extremely important. You should dress neatly, arrive on time, and smile. The job seeker should be able to answer questions such as the following:

- "Why do you want to work here?"
- "What skills or interests do you possess that make you a good fit for this position?"
- "What experiences have you had that show your strengths?"
- "What would you like to be doing in five years?"

Starting a Business

Most teenagers are excited to go to work for an established business. A few are especially adventurous. Even while they're in school, they decide to start their own businesses and be their own bosses.

In most cases, student businesses are solo services. A teenager may be a good musician and become an instructor, setting up a schedule of private lessons—usually taught at the instructor's home. For some, babysitting or after-school child care (being a nanny) is a steady service. Computer whizzes can become after-school and weekend consultants, performing certain computer tasks and solving technical problems for

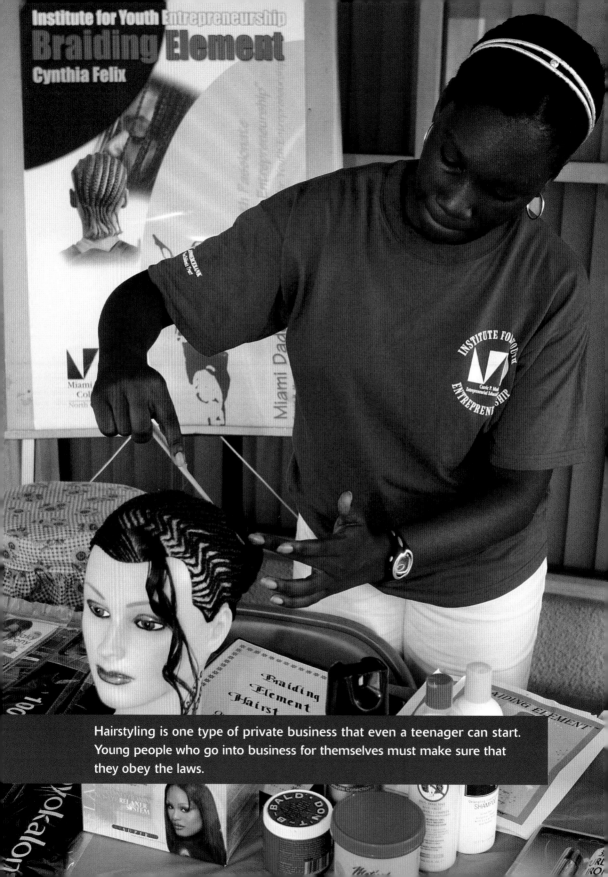

Hairstyling is one type of private business that even a teenager can start. Young people who go into business for themselves must make sure that they obey the laws.

local businesses and individuals. Photography buffs may land freelance assignments from newspapers and magazines. The founder of such a service might have a partner who shares expenses, income, and tasks, but rarely hires employees.

Some services involve little or no overhead or out-of-pocket expenses. Others require basic tools (a computer, software, and attachments, perhaps). They may require travel (gasoline and auto maintenance are significant expenses). Advertising might be necessary, at least in the beginning.

In all businesses, the owner must have an effective system for collecting money, must keep accurate records, and must obey tax requirements. The more successful and complex the business, the more likely the worker will need a tax professional to make sure the operation follows all laws and regulations. A financial adviser also can explain which expenses are tax-deductible.

CHAPTER 2

"How Much Can I Earn?"

Most first jobs do not make employees rich. Teenagers in the workforce are among the lowest-paid. The main reason is that most of them perform work that requires little prior experience. They receive the training they need on the job. But everyone starts with a first job, and the experience gained from it will help you get better-paying jobs in the future.

The Minimum Wage

The minimum wage is the least amount that employers are required to pay their workers. The U.S. Department of Labor enforces the national minimum wage. At the time that the Fair Minimum Wage Act of 2007 became federal law, the federal minimum wage was $5.15 per hour. This law called for increases each July 24 for the following three years. The minimum wage increased to $5.85 per hour in July 2007, to $6.55 per hour in July 2008, and to $7.25 per hour in July 2009.

Under the U.S. Department of Labor's Youth Minimum Wage Program, workers under age twenty can be paid substantially less than the federal minimum wage during the first ninety calendar days (in other words, not just work days) of employment. Their minimum wage during the trial period is $4.25 per hour. After three months (or beginning on their twentieth birthday, whichever occurs first), they must be paid the standard minimum wage.

Many states have their own minimum wage laws. About half the states have set minimum wage levels higher than that of the federal government. Seven states have lower minimum wages than the national requirement. The others either follow the federal

Higher Wages Better Jobs
A New Direction For **America**

U.S. House Speaker Nancy Pelosi and Senate Majority Leader Harry Reid celebrate the new minimum wage law at a rally in Washington, D.C.

guidelines or set no minimum wage at all. In states that have minimum wages different from that of the U.S. government, the higher wage is enforced.

Not every worker qualifies to receive the minimum wage. Many agricultural jobs are not covered. The law does not cover certain individuals who have disabilities that prevent them from being fully productive.

A special law applies to full-time students. Their employers are required to pay only 85 percent of the minimum wage.

Also under special terms are "student-learners." These are high school students who are taking vocational courses. Employers in their areas of training can hire them at a lower wage (70 percent of the minimum wage). In return, the employers provide them, while still in high school, with on-the-job experience that will help them get good jobs when they graduate.

Differing Pay Scales

Some jobs involve odd pay structures that can change an employee's income greatly from day to day and month to

A young sales clerk *(left)* helps a shopper at a Florida clothing store. Such jobs provide excellent experience in interacting with the public. Many salespeople receive hourly wages, commissions, or a combination of the two methods of compensation.

month. People in sales, for example, usually work on commission. They are paid a percentage of the amount they sell. Commission percentages vary, and sales trends go up and down. Sometimes, the salesperson can sell a product very quickly. Then, it may be days or weeks before another sale is made.

Suppose a seller of furniture is working on a commission of 10 percent. One day, the salesperson sells $1,000 worth of furniture. Ten percent of $1,000 is $100. If the person works approximately eight hours per day, the earnings on that day would be $12.50 per hour ($100 divided by eight hours). The next day, the person sells only $100 worth of furniture, receiving a commission of $10 (10 percent of $100). That means the person earns only $1.25 per hour on that day ($10 divided by eight hours).

Because sales patterns can be unpredictable, many companies pay their sales staff a salary plus commission. Depending on the business, the salary might be as low as the minimum wage. On the other hand, some companies pay very well to keep good salespeople happy during downturns in sales.

Some salespeople earn hundreds of thousands of dollars each year. Others don't earn enough to survive. Young people interested in sales jobs should be aware of the risks. They should think twice before taking a sales job that pays only a commission. They should also be wary of unknown companies that promise unbelievably high earnings.

Another class of wage earner with a special pay scale is the tipped employee, most notably waitstaff. Federal law requires the employer to pay only $2.13 per hour, apart from tips—assuming certain conditions are met. The law requires that this base pay plus tips must add up to at least the minimum wage. If it doesn't, the employer must increase the base pay. Some states have laws requiring a higher base pay for tipped workers.

Tipped employees in some situations do extremely well. Some of them earn many times more money in tips than they draw in base pay.

A Good Job Pays Much More Than Money

A really good job gives employees good benefits. Many smart job searchers are as interested in the benefits package as they are in the pay.

A typical benefit is health insurance. Group (company) health insurance benefits vary widely. Some employers'

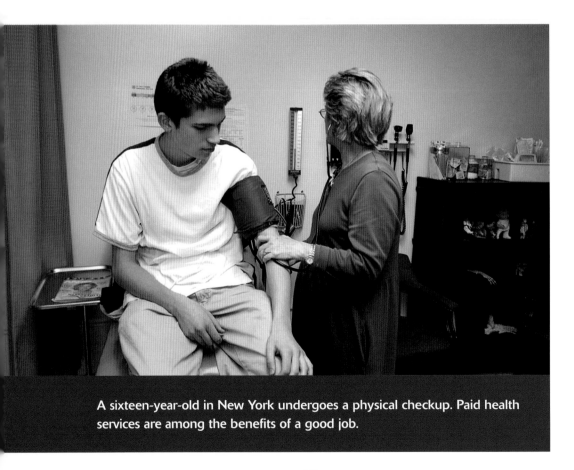

A sixteen-year-old in New York undergoes a physical checkup. Paid health services are among the benefits of a good job.

insurance policies cover almost everything for their employees. They may include long-term hospitalization, regular medical checkups, and full dental and vision care. Other policies cover only medical emergencies. Health policies also differ in the amount of deductible that the worker must pay. For example, the employee may have to pay the first $200, $500, or $1,000 of any medical expense; the insurance company will pay the rest. In many instances, that means the employee must pay the total cost. If an emergency room visit costs $800 and the policy's deductible is $500, the injured employee must pay $500 and the insurer pays only the remaining $300. But if a long-term hospitalization costs $50,000, most patients will gladly pay the $500 deductible.

Some companies also provide life insurance. These policies might pay a year's salary—or several years' salary—to the spouse or family if the employee dies.

Many employers pay or help pay for employee retirement plans like 401(k)s. In 401(k) accounts, the employee's taxes are put off until withdrawal, and he or she usually chooses the types of investments that are in the account. Some employers pay a share of investment programs.

Paid vacation and personal leave/sick time (in addition to holidays) are other important benefits. In most workplaces, employees get increasing amounts of annual leave the longer they stay with the company. Many employers offer maternity leave (time off from work for a mother who has just had a child) at full pay. Some provide free family, financial, and legal counseling to employees who need it.

Increasingly, employers are giving their workers unex-pected perks. They might treat everyone to picnics, ski trips, and Friday matinee movies—all expenses paid. The cost to the employer is small compared to the employee loyalty and job satisfaction that result.

Myths and Facts

Myth   High school and college students don't have to pay taxes.

Fact   They do have to pay taxes if they earn above a certain amount of money in a year. They need to know the tax requirements of both their state and federal governments.

Myth   Teenagers are paid at least the minimum wage.

Fact   Many of them are. But by federal law, for their first ninety days on the job, they can be paid substantially less. Full-time students and student-learners may also receive less than the minimum wage.

Myth   It's better to find a job as waitstaff than as a cashier or restaurant host/hostess. Waitstaff don't have to pay taxes on the tips they make.

Fact   It may be a better job simply because tipped employees often enjoy remarkable incomes. However, they have to pay taxes on all of their earnings. They report their tips to their employer, who in turn reports the annual total to state and federal tax agencies. A server who is hiding tips is breaking the law.

Chapter 3
Full-Time, Part-Time, or Seasonal Time?

If you are serious about working, you have probably done the math before beginning your job search. For example, you have calculated: "If I can get a job that pays $7 an hour and I work ten hours a week, I'll earn $70 a week. That's enough (or not enough) for me while I'm in school." "If I can work twenty hours a week after school and on weekends, I'll earn $140 a week. That's enough (or not enough) not only to buy the things I want and to save a lot of money, but also to help my parents pay some bills."

There are only two factors in this simple formula: hourly wage and number of hours. You, as a teen, won't find a very wide range in hourly wages. For most student jobs, roughly minimum wage, give or take a dollar an hour, is what you can expect to be paid. The number of hours worked, then, is the main factor in determining how much you will earn.

Before committing to any job, you must carefully weigh work time against other responsibilities. Time for schoolwork is most important. So is time for after-school clubs or sports. Time for household chores must be considered. A

Many students choose to commit most of their free time to hobbies, sports, clubs, or other extracurricular activities at school, rather than take on a job.

certain amount of downtime—time for recreation, friends, and family—is necessary each week. And, of course, you have to sleep sometime. In the end, you must decide which pursuits are most important during the teen years. How much time are you willing to devote to work?

Child Labor Laws

When a teenager becomes eighteen, there are no employment age requirements under law. (Some types of jobs require that a worker be at least twenty-one to hold the job.) Until then,

A guidance counselor at a Virginia school consults with a student. Counselors can explain state and federal laws and other requirements involved in different types of employment.

students may be limited in the number of hours they can work and in the kinds of jobs they can hold. Besides laws that are enforced by the U.S. Department of Labor, some states enforce special child labor laws. Because labor laws change and vary from state to state, teenagers should ask their school guidance counselors about their employment options.

Basically, employees ages sixteen and seventeen can work any number of hours, except in jobs that the Department of Labor considers unsafe. (Power saws, mixing and grinding devices, and other types of equipment can make a workplace unsafe under child labor laws.) You might qualify for a payroll job at age fourteen or fifteen, but work hours will be limited: no more than three hours per day, eighteen hours per week during the school term (full-time work is allowed in summer). Most fourteen- and fifteen-year-olds are not allowed to work later than 7:00 PM when school is in session or later than 9:00 PM even in summer. Teenagers who work under terms of the Department of Labor's full-time student program can work no more than eight hours a day, twenty hours a week, during the school term. (They can work forty-hour weeks during summer and winter breaks.)

There are exceptions to the general rules. For instance, in most cases, children younger than fourteen are allowed to work in shops, stores, and restaurants owned by their parents. Child entertainers (in radio, TV, movies, or stage presentations) are not subject to Fair Labor Standards Act time limitations.

Managing Your Time

Regardless of the laws, you should think about your time very carefully before entering the workforce. Going to work is a life change for you. A job that involves weeknight work obviously interferes with regular homework time. Can you find time to

Summer and Holiday Jobs

Some students, after carefully considering how they want to spend their time, decide to limit their employment to summer and seasonal jobs. Many employers hire more teenagers during the summer, when their full-time adult workers take vacation time. Holiday periods also present good opportunities for young workers, especially in retail stores where shopping is at a mad pace.

If they learn to save their seasonal earnings and manage their money wisely, teenagers can stretch their short-term incomes to meet their spending needs throughout the year. Holiday work doesn't interfere with their studies. And when school is out of session, they can work full-time hours.

complete assignments (before going to work after school, late at night, early in the morning before classes begin)? Will this be too stressful?

It will be helpful to find a first job that offers an adaptable work schedule. If no flextime is available, you will have to arrange the rest of your life around the job.

Above all, the first job will force you to learn a new kind of discipline. Frequently arriving late for work will likely cause you to lose the job. So will slack performance. A bad attitude about the work, unfriendliness toward other employees, and constant clock-watching are unlikely to lead to promotions. Getting fired from a job definitely will not look good on a résumé. If you are

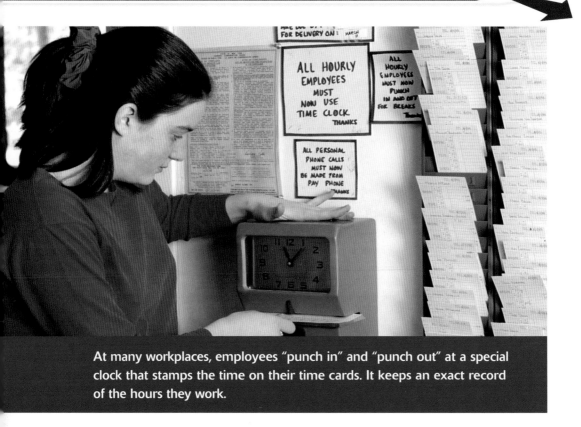

At many workplaces, employees "punch in" and "punch out" at a special clock that stamps the time on their time cards. It keeps an exact record of the hours they work.

unhappy, the best remedy is to continue performing as well as possible while seeking a new job. If a new job cannot be found, resign while you are still on good terms with the management. In the long run, it's best for you to bow out of the situation gracefully than to be dismissed for poor performance.

CHAPTER 4

"What Do I Do with All This Money?"

What do you do with all that money? First, do not blow it. Budget it.

A simple budget shows income and expenses from week to week, month to month, or paycheck to paycheck. Income is how much money a person receives. The expense part of the budget worksheet shows each payment for each purchase. A good budget should be able to tell you exactly how every dollar is spent. A solid understanding of that is necessary to avoid financial trouble.

The Hard Truth About Money

Until you begin a job and create a budget, personal finances—the income and outgo of money—are vague. The budget is like a bright light that illuminates the good and the bad things about income and expenses. A budget is a changing picture. It is regularly adjusted with new information. Every time money is received or spent, it changes the budget.

Many people examine their budget reports at the end of every month. Some revise their budgets each week. The most devoted budget keepers

Preparing and maintaining a budget shows a worker how much money is earned and how it is spent. A careful budget is the basis of good money management.

look at their worksheets every day. For others, it makes the best sense to review the budget at the end of each pay period.

Whatever budget period you want to use, the objective is to balance the budget. In a balanced budget, expenses never exceed income. If spending is more than income during any given budget period, the situation must be corrected quickly. If it isn't, a short-term budget problem can grow into a financial crisis that might take years to untangle.

An example of a balanced monthly budget is as follows:

October 2009

Income

Marko Theater Company	$ 211.25
Total income	$ 211.25

Expenses

ice cream	$ 3.00
music downloads	$ 20.00
birthday gift for Dana	$ 21.00
clothes	$ 58.00
lunch with friends	$ 6.00
gas	$ 40.00
cosmetics	$ 15.00
dinner with friends	$ 12.00
Total expenses	$175.00

Cash on hand

($211.25 − 175.00 = $36.25)	$ 36.25

The following is an example of an unbalanced monthly budget:

November 2009
Income
Marko Theater Company	$ 196.14

Total income	$ 196.14

Expenses
movie	$ 7.50
DVD purchase	$ 20.00
music downloads	$ 9.00
dinner with friends	$ 10.00
bargain DVD purchase	$ 6.00
T-shirt	$ 13.50
shoes	$ 45.00
two pairs of jeans	$ 70.00
lunch with friends	$ 7.00
gas	$ 38.00
cosmetics	$ 15.00
dinner with friends	$ 12.00

Total expenses	$253.00

Overspending amount
($196.14 - $253.00 = -$56.86)	-$ 56.86

Notice that every expense should be entered separately into the budget worksheet. Do not fail to enter minor expenses. It's a good idea to record the dates of income checks and expenses.

If you are spending more than earning, the situation must be reversed. Solutions: spend less and/or earn more. Few people can afford everything they would like to buy. A simple budget reveals why.

Budgeting teaches a young worker the importance of wise shopping. Few people can buy everything they want. But with discipline and common sense, they can stretch their paychecks.

Every sound budget will have an additional line item not shown in these examples: savings deposit. Beginning with your first job, you should commit to saving a specific amount from each paycheck. During budget periods when the numbers look particularly bright, more money can go into savings.

A budget is also a valuable planning tool. A person who wants to make a special purchase can determine in advance if (and when) it is affordable. This is done by calculating expected income and expenses for the next budget period and comparing them with recent budget reports. The results will probably present various possibilities, such as the following:

- "Should be no problem. I can buy it right now."
- "If I work four extra hours this month and keep my expenses at the same level as last month, I can afford it."
- "If I don't eat out or buy any clothes this month, I can afford it."
- "There's no way I can afford this right now without getting into serious money trouble."

Processing Your Paycheck

When they receive their paychecks, most workers take them to their banks and deposit them into their checking accounts. (More and more employees are having their employers deposit their earnings directly into their bank accounts via electronic transfers instead of receiving a physical check or cash.) Workers might do several other things with the money from the paycheck at that time. They may take out a small amount of cash for their wallets. Those who are wise deposit a portion of their earnings into savings accounts.

If they can afford to, they can put some of their income into investments.

Young people cannot open checking accounts until they are eighteen years old, unless an adult cosigns the account. That means the adult agrees to be responsible for the account if the teenager acts recklessly. For example, if the young customer has $500 in the checking account and writes checks amounting to $600 without depositing more money, the account is overdrawn by $100. After an account becomes overdrawn, the bank will refuse to honor the checks that are written. It will "bounce" them back to the businesses or individuals to whom they were paid. It's costly to overdraw a checking account and bounce checks. The account holder must deposit funds into the checking account before it can be used again. Worse, the customer will probably have to pay an overdraft fee to the bank, plus a returned-check fee to the victim of the bounce. The incident can stain the person's credit record. A history of check bouncing can hurt the individual's future attempts to obtain credit and get a job.

On the other hand, a teenager can open a savings account at a younger age. There is no danger of overdrafts with a savings account because there is no check writing. The customer must go to the bank to withdraw money, or request the bank by phone or online to move funds from the savings account to a different account. The bank will not transfer more money from savings than the customer has available in the account.

Why Save? Why Invest?

Some working teenagers have only savings accounts. Each time they receive a paycheck, they keep some of the money in

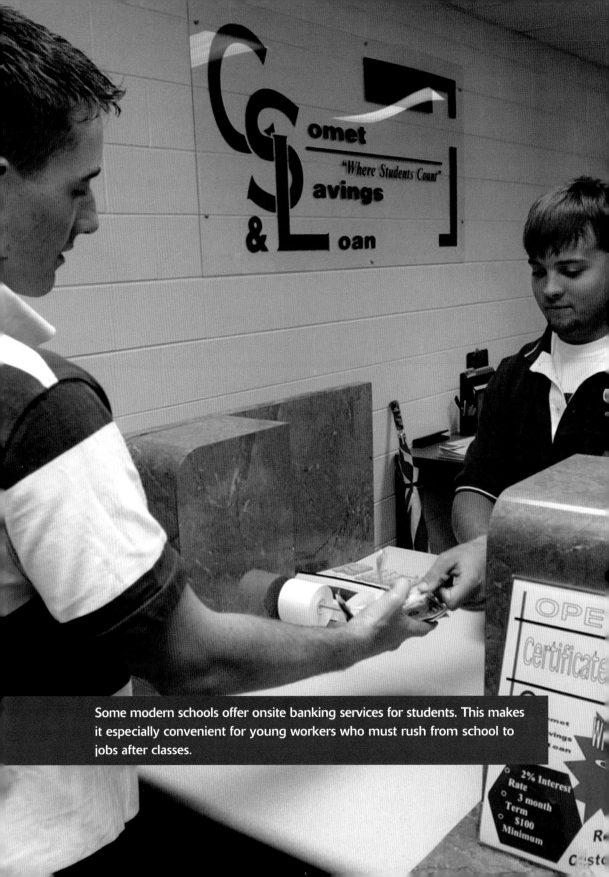

Some modern schools offer onsite banking services for students. This makes it especially convenient for young workers who must rush from school to jobs after classes.

cash for spending but deposit most of it into savings. Unless they really need to pay for things frequently by check, it's a smart way to handle the income from their first job. It's exciting to watch a savings account grow. What makes it even more exciting is something called interest.

When customers deposit money into savings accounts for long periods of time, the bank uses the money to make loans to other people. When those people pay back the borrowed money, they must pay the bank an additional fee—the interest on the loan. The bank, in turn, pays a small percentage of interest to its customers who have savings accounts. It does not pay its savers nearly as much in interest as it charges its borrowers. (That is how the bank makes money.) For example, it may charge an interest rate of 5 or 10 percent (or higher) on a loan. It may pay less than 1 percent interest to savings account holders. But the interest for the saver adds up. And since interest earned is a percentage of the money that you have in the bank, the more money you deposit, the more interest you can earn.

There is a way to earn even more interest with savings. Money can be invested in a special, long-term account. In an investment account, the bank customer agrees to leave money in a special bank account for a year, five years, ten years, or longer. The customer cannot withdraw the money during the investment period without being charged an early-withdrawal fee. However, in the end, the investment can earn the customer several times more interest than a regular savings account. For young employees who are saving much of their incomes and who know they won't need the money for a while, investing is wise money management.

Many forms of investment are available. Banks can set up money market accounts based on international stock markets.

New Conveniences, New Risks

Identity theft has alarmed workers and consumers in recent years. Stalkers have been known to swipe personal identification information from citizens' street garbage. Far more clever stalkers use the Internet, looking for weaknesses in Web browser and e-mail systems that

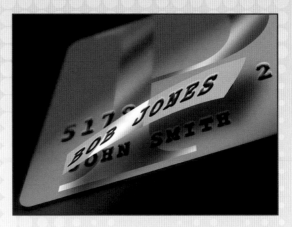

Identity theft is a serious and growing problem. Skeptics worry that online shopping and banking make society more susceptible to electronic crime.

let them into the personal computers and private lives of unsuspecting individuals.

Some Internet observers claim it is at least as safe—possibly safer—to do business online as on paper. Others believe the Internet has opened a can of worms when it comes to financial security. Hackers, they warn, can obtain every detail from the user's Social Security number to banking and credit card account numbers.

Every expert agrees that a computer security program is needed if a worker plans to bank online. That includes security of the user's Web browser. But will software security be enough? The question lingers.

Some employers encourage their workers by establishing individual retirement accounts (IRAs) and 401(k) plans. Many workers buy stocks or bonds. A financial adviser is strongly recommended to sort out the options for employees who are interested in long-term investing.

Note that most investments require that the customer deposit a large amount of money for a long period of time. That makes it difficult for many teenage employees to become investors. The typical way to break into investing is to start a standard savings account. When the account balance exceeds $1,000, consider converting some or all of the savings to a long-term investment.

Electronic Money

Many people believe that all finances are going electronic and online. For years, shoppers have been ordering products online. They have paid with their credit or debit cards. The payment goes into the seller's bank account. Neither the buyer nor the seller ever touches real money.

Increasingly, many people now prefer to pay their bills over the Internet. It is very fast and easy. It is also automated. That means the same payment process is repeated each month. The customer enters the new monthly payment numbers, clicks once or twice with the computer mouse, and the computer system does the rest. The customer might allow a phone company, utility company, or insurance company to withdraw monthly payments automatically from his or her checking account. The customer never has to write and mail a check.

Similarly, an advantage of having paychecks directly deposited is fast processing. If they receive paychecks in person on the fifteenth of the month, it might be the sixteenth or later until employees can get to their banks and deposit

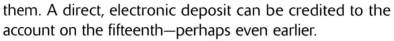

them. A direct, electronic deposit can be credited to the account on the fifteenth—perhaps even earlier.

Some say the Internet has made paper and metal money objects of the past. Do people really need coins and bills? Almost every purchase and payment can be made with a plastic credit or debit card, or processed automatically by employers and banks.

Skeptics raise a simple, chilling question: what will happen to people's finances if the Internet fails? For that reason, most workers prefer to have cash in their hands at all times.

Chapter 5

Paying the Government and Giving Back to Society

Do teenagers have to pay taxes, either on a part-time or a full-time job? Usually, yes. The Internal Revenue Service (IRS), a branch of the U.S. Department of the Treasury, provides information on tax requirements for all categories of wage earners. In addition to paying the federal government, workers must pay taxes to the states in which they live.

A worker who is self-employed must keep track of how much of the earnings should go to state and federal governments. The individual makes estimated tax payments to state and federal tax agencies each quarter. At the end of the year, the person (or a tax professional) calculates the total income, deductible expenses, and taxes that were due. If the individual has paid more in quarterly estimates than was necessary, a tax refund should result. If the self-employed worker underpaid in quarterly estimates, he or she must pay the remainder by April 15.

Most workers are employed by businesses. The employer withholds a share of state and federal taxes from each paycheck. The amount

What Does the Government Do with These Withholdings?

Employees' tax dollars pay for a wide variety of public services. Part of the money pays for national defense. Part of it pays for social services—to help support Americans who can't find work, are unable to work, or need other types of assistance. It pays for law enforcement and prison facilities. It pays to keep roads in good condition, to widen some of them because of increasing traffic, and to build new ones. It pays for public education. It pays for government research in science and other areas. It pays government office holders' salaries and benefits. Many other public programs and services are also funded by workers' taxes.

Social Security is what the federal government describes as "a system of social insurance." A small portion of an employee's earnings goes into the system; the employer must pay a matching amount. The Social Security Administration uses this money to pay benefits to older workers who have retired. Eventually, when today's young worker reaches retirement age, the paycheck deductions of future workers will pay the current worker's own retirement benefits. Retirees are not the only beneficiaries of Social Security. Children whose parents are retired or disabled might receive Social Security money. Injured workers can receive disability pay.

Medicare is a similar federal program. It helps pay for the medical needs of people who are ages sixty-five and older, especially for hospital stays, doctor bills, medicine, and related expenses.

withheld (which the employer pays to the government on behalf of the employee) is based on tax formulas for the current year. At the end of the year, the employee (or a tax professional) must calculate total earnings, taxes paid, and possible deductions. It may be that the worker can deduct certain job-related expenses. In that case, the employee should receive a tax refund.

Understanding Your Paycheck

Most paychecks include a stub, which is an attached form that the employee keeps as a record. It shows details about how the pay was processed. You should notice first the "gross pay" and "net pay" entries. Gross pay is the total amount the employer pays. If you have clocked ten hours during the pay period and are being paid $10 an hour, the gross pay will be $100 (ten hours times $10).

However, the paycheck probably will be for a lower amount—the net pay. The employer takes out federal and state taxes (including state unemployment and state disability insurance), Social Security, Medicare, and possibly other deductions. (For instance, you may be responsible for paying a portion of the company insurance plan.) After subtracting them all, the net pay—the amount of the check—results. This is commonly known as the take-home pay. The pay stub will usually indicate not just what the deductions are for the current pay period but the amount of deductions for the whole year, up to that point. The label "YTD" in any section of the pay stub means "year to date"—the amount of earnings or deductions since the beginning of the year.

The pay stub shows the beginning and ending dates of the pay period, the employee's name and tax status (dependent, single, married, etc.), and probably an employee number.

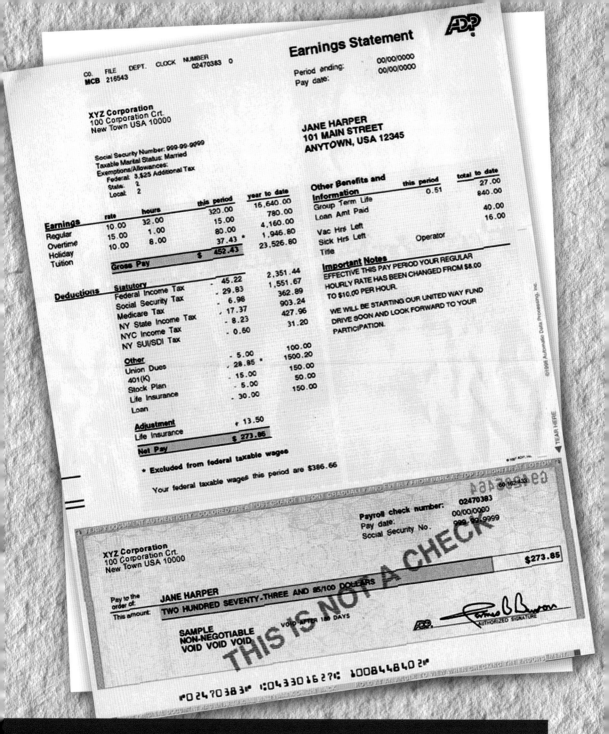

A paycheck stub or "earnings statement" shows the worker details about hours worked, amount paid, and different types of withholdings.

Some employers provide very detailed pay stubs. They might keep track of vacation and sick leave, for example. If the employee has the money directly deposited into a personal checking or savings account, that information (including the account number) will be shown.

Complicated Rules

Not all teenagers are subject to identical tax requirements. In most families, a parent can claim one or more children as dependents. This means the parents can claim a special tax deduction on their own earnings because of the usual costs of supporting a dependent child. A dependent child who gets a

Workers and job seekers can learn about tax requirements at the Web sites of the Internal Revenue Service (www.irs.gov) and state tax agencies.

job may or may not have to file a separate tax return each year. It depends largely on the amount of the child's earned income (wages, salary, or—if self-employed—fees received). Unearned income, such as savings account interest, is also a factor.

The IRS (www.irs.gov) provides details about federal tax requirements on its Web site. For information about a state's requirements, you should find the Web site of the state's department of revenue or taxes. A school guidance counselor can provide basic information about tax requirements for you. Tax professionals and financial advisers can also provide detailed information about your specific situation.

Even when the federal law exempts a teenager from filing a tax return, the IRS advises that you file a return in certain situations. For example, if you had income tax withheld from paychecks, you might qualify for a tax refund.

Give Back to Society

Earning money is a good feeling. Giving some of it to worthy causes is an even nicer feeling. At an early age, you should consider giving a portion of the paycheck back to society.

Needy organizations and individuals are everywhere. You may choose to give a biblical tithe (tenth) to a church. The Red Cross and other relief organizations constantly need funds. Nonprofit agencies seek contributions to protect the environment, feed hungry people in third world countries (and in poverty-stricken areas of the United States), and raise money for people with special needs. They also preserve historic landmarks and support the arts.

There are countless community causes, too. For example, a high school band may be raising funds for an appearance in the Thanksgiving Day parade in New York or for new

These student athletes in Maryland helped raise funds for the American Red Cross shortly after Hurricane Katrina ravaged the Gulf Coast. Consider giving back to society by contributing some of your earnings to worthy causes.

instruments. A neighborhood organization may want street beautification. Or, a civic club will sponsor a trip to Disney World for area children with muscular dystrophy if it can raise enough money.

Some contributions are tax-deductible. When it comes time to file annual tax returns, the giver can subtract those contributions from the income that is reported to the government and pay less taxes. To some contributors, it does not matter whether the donation is deductible or not; the cause is what's important. Still, it makes sense to find out if any contribution can result in savings at April tax time.

CHAPTER 6

Beginning of a Career?

Your first job is a landmark in life. If it is performed well and provides valuable experience—a stepping-stone to better employment—it will probably appear on your résumé until you retire. Even at mid-career, job applicants can describe their first job proudly as part of their accomplishments.

At least as important are the life skills— especially financial skills—the first job will bring. You will either learn to become a smart income manager or squander much of the hard-earned money and look back in disappointment in later years.

Even though your first job may not be what you want to do for a living, it can be a first step toward a career. Many students by high school graduation have a vague idea where they want to go with their vocations. Most college students by graduation have a much clearer plan. They are actively exploring the job market and already may have obtained related work experience.

"Whistle While You Work"

"Whistle While You Work" is the title of a classic song from the *Snow White* animated movie. It

A teenage worker serves a retirement home resident in New York. A cheerful attitude is an important trait of an employee in any job setting.

has to do with a person's attitude. If possible, you should look for a first job that will be enjoyable. All jobs require workers to perform boring or difficult tasks sometimes. Unless it is truly necessary, though, you should resist pursuing a job opportunity simply for the purpose of making money. You should seek a first job in which you look forward to going to work. At the same time, a job should begin teaching you about the business side of life and, if possible, provide experience toward your future career path.

Even if it pays well, a bad first job can have negative financial effects in the long run. It can dampen your desire to stand out and advance. It can create an early impression that a job is something to be endured, not enjoyed. The result can be a lifelong cycle of unsatisfying employment. If you are not motivated to do your best, your prospects for promotions and other job opportunities are poor. So, try to find a job that you will enjoy doing.

Keep the Job Until You Find a Better One

If you find a good job, you will want to keep it. You will work hard and demonstrate honesty, reliability, and a cheerful attitude. Meanwhile, you will be acquiring life skills that can be obtained only in the workplace. These include time management and money management. During the months or years of employment, you can be building a nice savings account and may even be making long-term investments.

A first job is almost never the last. The time will come for you to move on—maybe before high school graduation. Ideally, when it's time to take a better job, you will leave on good terms with the first employer. The first employer can be an important reference for many years to come. However, as time passes, the employer might close the business or move

Ten Great Questions to Ask
A Financial Adviser

1 Do I have to pay taxes on money I earn before I'm twenty-one? Before I'm eighteen? Before I'm fourteen?

2 Do I have to pay taxes on money I earn doing odd jobs (mowing lawns, babysitting, teaching guitar or tennis, taking care of neighbors' pets, tutoring)?

3 If I become a salesperson and work totally on commission, will I have to pay taxes?

4 Am I limited in the number of hours I can work each week until I reach a certain age?

5 How old must I be before I can get a "real job," with a regular paycheck?

6 My cousin in another state works for the same fast-food restaurant chain I work for. We have the same job title, perform the same tasks, and receive the same hourly wage. A higher percentage of my earnings is withheld than hers. Why?

7 What are some things I can do to make part of my income tax-exempt?

8 How old must I be before I can start my own company or professional service?

9 What types of employee benefits should I expect in my first job?

10 Do I need an accountant or tax professional to make sure I don't get in trouble with the government?

away. It's a good idea for you to obtain a letter of reference from the first boss. The letter should be dated and addressed "To Whom It May Concern," and it will hopefully contain a glowing recommendation to any future employer.

A first job is the beginning of an individual's working life. It could lead to a career; it might not. A sixteen-year-old who lands a job as a supermarket checkout clerk might go on to become a psychologist. A seventeen-year-old who runs errands for a law firm might go on to become a supermarket manager. On the other hand, a teenager who works after school as a veterinarian's assistant just might go on to become a veterinarian.

A veterinary staff member treats a horse that requires surgery. Some young people are able to find part-time jobs as assistants to professionals in their intended career fields.

Whatever the job, it's an important first step for you. You should learn as much from the experience as possible. Almost always, it will teach priceless lessons about money.

And there's one special thing about your first job: you never forget it.

Glossary

benefits Job attractions in addition to pay, including financial assistance in case of emergencies and retirement, paid vacation time, and other rewards.

bond A type of investment in which an individual helps the government, or a corporation, pay for a special project and earns interest in return.

budget A financial system that shows an individual, company, or organization how much money comes in and exactly how it is spent.

credit record The history and rating of how a person handles debts.

deductible An amount of a health or damage insurance claim that the insured person must pay before the insurance company begins its coverage; also, an expense that lowers taxable income.

deposit To put money into a bank account.

direct deposit The electronic deposit of a paycheck by an employer into an employee's bank account.

exempt Free of obligation; not required to obey certain laws or rules.

income Money a person receives in the form of paychecks, gifts, and sales.

interest A percentage of a borrowed amount of money that must be paid to the lender or investor, in addition to the original amount.

invest To put part of one's income into a financial plan that eventually will pay a high rate of interest.

IRA Individual retirement account; part of a worker's pay that is automatically deducted and invested in a special savings account.

money market account A savings account that usually pays higher interest than a regular savings account.

overdraft An amount of money written from a checking account that exceeds the balance available in the account.

overhead Ongoing business expenses, such as leasing office space and paying for water and electricity services.

salary Income earned from employment.

stock market A place where stocks are bought and sold by investors.

stock Part of the ownership of a company, also known as a share.

tax exemption A portion of earnings on which taxes do not have to be paid.

tax refund The government's year-end return to a citizen of tax money that was overpaid from payroll deductions during the year.

wage The amount a worker is paid by the hour.

For More Information

Canadian Legal Information Institute
360 Albert Street, Suite 1700
Ottawa, ON K1R 7X7
Canada
Web site: http://www.canlii.org
This institute provides information about Canadian labor laws.
    See especially the "Canada Labor Code" section (http://
    www.canlii.org/ca/sta/l-2/index.html).

Human Resources and Social Development Canada
    Labor Program
Human Resources and Social Development Canada
Ottawa, ON K1A 0J2
Canada
Web site: http://www.hrsdc.gc.ca/en/labour/index.shtml
This is Canada's federal labor department. See especially the
    document "Minimum Age for Employment in Canada"
    (http://www.hrsdc.gc.ca/en/lp/spila/clli/eslc/minage(e).pdf).

Internal Revenue Service (IRS)
U.S. Department of the Treasury
1500 Pennsylvania Avenue NW
Washington, DC 202220
(202) 622-2000
Web site: http://www.irs.gov
The IRS is the branch of the Treasury Department that over-
    sees taxes.

U.S. Bureau of Labor Statistics (BLS)
2 Massachusetts Avenue NE

Washington, DC 20212-0001
(202) 691-5200
Web site: http://www.bls.gov
A labor fact-finding and economics agency within the U.S.
    Department of Labor, the BLS has a "Jobseeker or
    Worker" resource section (http://www.bls.gov/audience/
    jobseekers.htm).

U.S. Department of Labor
Frances Perkins Building
200 Constitution Avenue NW
Washington, DC 20210
(866) 487-2365
Web site: http://www.dol.gov
This is the federal government agency that is responsible for
    enforcing labor laws.

U.S. Occupational Safety & Health Administration
200 Constitution Avenue NW
Washington, DC 20210
(800) 321-6742
Web site: http://www.osha.gov
This department provides job safety information. See especially
    the section for teenage employees (http://www.osha.gov/
    SLTC/teenworkers/index.html).

U.S. Social Security Administration
Office of Public Inquiries
Windsor Park Building
6401 Security Boulevard
Baltimore, MD 21235
(800) 772-1213

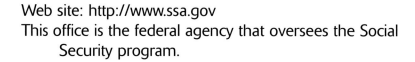

Web site: http://www.ssa.gov
This office is the federal agency that oversees the Social
        Security program.

Web Sites

Due to the changing nature of Internet links, Rosen Publishing
has developed an online list of Web sites related to the subject
of this book. This site is updated regularly. Please use this link
to access the list:

http://www.rosenlinks.com/gsm/job

For Further Reading

Bolles, Richard Nelson, Carol Christen, and Jean M. Blomquiest. *What Color Is Your Parachute for Teens: Discovering Yourself, Defining Your Future.* Berkeley, CA: Ten Speed Press, 2006.

Brancato Robin. *Money: The Ultimate Teen Guide.* Blue Ridge Summit, PA: The Scarecrow Press, 2006.

Byers, Ann. *Great Resume, Application, and Interview Skills* (Work Readiness). New York, NY: Rosen Publishing, 2008.

Cauvier, Denis, and Alan Lysaght. *The ABCs of Making Money 4 Teens.* Ogdensburg, NY: Wealth Solutions Press, 2005.

Coon, Nora. *Teen Dream Jobs: How to Find the Job You Really Want Now!* Hillsboro, OR: Beyond Words, 2003.

Denega, Danielle. *Smart Money: How to Manage Your Cash.* London, England: Franklin Watts, 2008.

Drobot, Eve. *Money, Money, Money: Where It Comes From, How to Save It, Spend It and Make It.* Toronto, ON: Maple Tree Press, Inc., 2004.

Giesecke, Ernestine. *Dollars and Sense: Managing Your Money.* Chicago, IL: Heinemann Library, 2003.

Holmberg, Joshua, and David Bruzzese. *The Teen's Guide to Personal Finance: Basic Concepts in Personal Finance That Every Teen Should Know.* Littleton, CO: iUniverse, 2008.

Reeves, Diane Lindsey, with Gayle Bryan. *Career Ideas for Kids Who Like Money.* 2nd ed. New York, NY: Checkmark Books, 2007.

Bibliography

Bureau of Labor Statistics. *Occupational Outlook Handbook, 2008-09 Edition*. U.S. Department of Labor. Retrieved August 29, 2008 (http://www.bls.gov/oco).

Doyle, Alison. "Child Labor Law." About.com. Retrieved September 20, 2008 (http://jobsearch.about.com/od/employmentlaw/a/childlaborlaw.htm).

Doyle, Alison. "Finding Your First Job." About.com. Retrieved September 20, 2008 (http://jobsearch.about.com/od/teenstudentgrad/a/firstjob.htm).

Doyle, Alison. "How to Apply for a Part-Time Job." About.com. Retrieved September 21, 2008 (http://jobsearch.about.com/od/parttimejobs/a/applyparttime.htm).

Doyle, Alison. "Teen Jobs—Teen Job Search." About.com. Retrieved September 20, 2008 (http://jobsearch.about.com/cs/justforstudents/a/teenjobs.htm).

Internal Revenue Service. *Publication 501: Exemptions, Standard Deduction and Filing Information*. Retrieved September 20, 2008 (http://www.irs.gov/publications/p501/ar02.html#d0e955).

Internal Revenue Service. "Tax Information for Students." Retrieved September 20, 2008 (http://www.irs.gov/individuals/students/index.html).

JIST Editors. *Exploring Careers: A Young Person's Guide to 1,000 Jobs*. 3rd Ed. Indianapolis, IN: JIST Publishing, Inc., 2003.

MSN. "Résumés & Cover Letters." MSN.careers. Retrieved September 21, 2008 (http://msn.careerbuilder.com/Custom/MSN/CareerAdvice/Category.aspx?categoryid=CL).

Ryan, Robin. "Dos and Don'ts of a Good Cover Letter."
    MSN.careers. Retrieved September 21, 2008 (http://
    msn.careerbuilder.com/custom/msn/careeradvice/
    viewarticle.aspx?articleid=1300&SiteId=cbmsn41300&sc_
    extcmp=JS_1300_advice&catid=cl).
SnagAJob.com. "Working Papers: Everything You Need to Find
    and Conquer Your First Job." Retrieved September 20,
    2008 (http://www.snagajob.com/uploadedfiles/SnagAJob.
    com-First-job-guide.pdf).
U.S. Department of Labor. "Wages: Minimum Wage." Retrieved
    September 18, 2008 (http://www.dol.gov/dol/topic/wages/
    minimumwage.html).
Ward, Mike. "Summer Jobs for Teens." SnagAJob.com.
    Retrieved September 20, 2008 (http://www.snagajob.
    com/job-resources/teen-summer-jobs.aspx).
Weiss, Jodi, and Russell Kahn. *145 Things to Be When You
    Grow Up: Planning a Successful Career While You're Still
    in High School*. New York, NY: Princeton Review
    Publishing, LLC, 2004.

Index

About the Author

Daniel E. Harmon is the author of more than sixty books and numerous articles for national and regional magazines and newspapers. *Careers in Explosives and Arson Investigation*, his book for Rosen Publishing's Careers in Forensics series, was published in 2008. *Careers in the Corrections System*, his book for Rosen Publishing's Careers in Criminal Justice series, was published in 2009. He lives in Spartanburg, South Carolina.

Photo Credits

Cover (silhouette) © www.istockphoto.com/Gene Chutka; cover, p. 1 (top, bottom) © www.istockphoto.com/dra_schwartz, (middle) © www.istockphoto.com/Robert Deal; pp. 7, 16, 23, 29, 41, 49 © www.istockphoto.com/Kirby Hamilton; pp. 4–5 © Tony Savino/The Image Works; p. 8 © www.istockphoto.com/Richard Cano; pp. 14, 18 © Jeff Greenberg/The Image Works; p. 17 Tim Sloan/AFP/Getty Images; p. 20 © Ellen B. Senisi/The Images Works; p. 24 © www.istockphoto.com/James Boulette; p. 25 © Spmda Dawes/The Images Works; p. 28 © Dion Ogust/The Image Works; p. 30 © www.istockphoto.com/Ieva Geneviciene; p. 33 © www.istockphoto.com/Elena Elisseeva; p. 36 © AP Images; p. 38 © Barry Blackman/SuperStock; p. 47 Doug Pensinger/Getty Images; p. 50 © Syracuse Newspapers/Li-Hau Lan/The Image Works; p. 53 Jens-Ulrich Koch/AFP/Getty Images.

Designer: Sam Zavieh; Editor: Kathy Kuhtz Campbell; Photo Researcher: Amy Feinberg